50 Beyond Sushi: Japan's Forgotten Rice Dishes

By: Kelly Johnson

Table of Contents

- **Kayaku Gohan** (Seasoned Mixed Rice)
- **Zosui** (Japanese Rice Porridge)
- **Takikomi Gohan** (Soy-Simmered Rice with Vegetables)
- **Kuri Gohan** (Chestnut Rice)
- **Tai Meshi** (Sea Bream Rice)
- **Imo Gohan** (Sweet Potato Rice)
- **Matsutake Gohan** (Pine Mushroom Rice)
- **Hamaguri Gohan** (Clam Rice)
- **Gomoku Gohan** (Five-Ingredient Mixed Rice)
- **Tori Meshi** (Chicken Rice)
- **Kaki Gohan** (Oyster Rice)
- **Anago Meshi** (Saltwater Eel Rice)
- **Saba Meshi** (Mackerel Rice)
- **Shirasu Gohan** (Whitebait Rice)
- **Sansai Gohan** (Mountain Vegetable Rice)
- **Buta Meshi** (Pork Rice)
- **Hiyashi Chazuke** (Cold Tea Rice)
- **Yuba Donburi** (Tofu Skin Rice Bowl)
- **Kitsune Donburi** (Fried Tofu Rice Bowl)
- **Oyako Donburi** (Chicken and Egg Rice Bowl)
- **Tamagotoji Donburi** (Scrambled Egg Rice Bowl)
- **Unadon** (Grilled Eel Rice Bowl)
- **Tekka Don** (Marinated Tuna Rice Bowl)
- **Niratama Don** (Garlic Chive and Egg Rice Bowl)
- **Tororo Gohan** (Grated Yam Rice)
- **Shiso Gohan** (Perilla Leaf Rice)
- **Yaki Onigiri** (Grilled Rice Balls)
- **Ishikari Gohan** (Salmon and Miso Rice)
- **Shimeji Gohan** (Shimeji Mushroom Rice)
- **Edamame Gohan** (Soybean Rice)
- **Satsuma Jiru Gohan** (Rice with Sweet Potato Soup)
- **Yuba Gohan** (Tofu Skin Steamed Rice)
- **Katsu Don** (Pork Cutlet Rice Bowl)
- **Niku Don** (Beef Rice Bowl)
- **Buri Daikon Gohan** (Yellowtail and Daikon Rice)

- **Karasumi Gohan** (Salted Mullet Roe Rice)
- **Satsuma-age Donburi** (Fried Fish Cake Rice Bowl)
- **Kibinago Gohan** (Silver-stripe Herring Rice)
- **Zuke Don** (Marinated Fish Rice Bowl)
- **Mentaiko Gohan** (Spicy Cod Roe Rice)
- **Kinoko Meshi** (Assorted Mushroom Rice)
- **Fukagawa Meshi** (Clam and Miso Rice)
- **Saba Misoni Gohan** (Miso-Braised Mackerel Rice)
- **Hakata Meshi** (Rice with Marinated Raw Fish)
- **Gobo Gohan** (Burdock Root Rice)
- **Tsukudani Gohan** (Rice with Preserved Soy-Simmered Fish)
- **Shiokara Gohan** (Salted Fermented Seafood Rice)
- **Chahan** (Japanese Fried Rice)
- **Omu Rice** (Omelette Rice)
- **Mochi Gohan** (Rice with Sticky Mochi Pieces)

Kayaku Gohan (Seasoned Mixed Rice)

Ingredients

- 1 cup short-grain rice
- 1 1/2 cups dashi broth
- 1/4 cup carrots, julienned
- 1/4 cup shiitake mushrooms, sliced
- 1/4 cup bamboo shoots, sliced
- 1 tbsp soy sauce
- 1 tbsp mirin

Instructions

1. Rinse rice and place it in a rice cooker or pot.
2. Add dashi broth, soy sauce, and mirin.
3. Mix in carrots, mushrooms, and bamboo shoots.
4. Cook as usual and let rest before serving.

Zosui (Japanese Rice Porridge)

Ingredients

- 2 cups leftover hot pot broth
- 1/2 cup cooked rice
- 1 egg, beaten
- 1/4 cup green onions, chopped
- 1/2 tsp soy sauce

Instructions

1. Bring hot pot broth to a simmer.
2. Add cooked rice and stir gently.
3. Slowly drizzle in beaten egg, stirring lightly.
4. Season with soy sauce and garnish with green onions.

Takikomi Gohan (Soy-Simmered Rice with Vegetables)

Ingredients

- 1 cup short-grain rice
- 1 1/2 cups dashi broth
- 1/4 cup shiitake mushrooms, sliced
- 1/4 cup carrots, julienned
- 1 tbsp soy sauce
- 1 tbsp mirin

Instructions

1. Rinse rice and place in a pot with dashi broth, soy sauce, and mirin.
2. Add mushrooms and carrots.
3. Cook on low heat for 20 minutes.
4. Let sit for 5 minutes before serving.

Kuri Gohan (Chestnut Rice)

Ingredients

- 1 cup short-grain rice
- 1 1/2 cups water
- 1/2 cup chestnuts, peeled and chopped
- 1/2 tsp salt

Instructions

1. Rinse rice and soak in water for 30 minutes.
2. Add chestnuts and salt, then cook as usual.
3. Let sit for 5 minutes before serving.

Tai Meshi (Sea Bream Rice)

Ingredients

- 1 cup short-grain rice
- 1 1/2 cups dashi broth
- 1 small whole sea bream (tai), cleaned
- 1 tbsp soy sauce
- 1 tbsp sake
- 1/4 cup green onions, chopped

Instructions

1. Rinse rice and place it in a pot with dashi, soy sauce, and sake.
2. Lay the whole sea bream on top.
3. Cook as usual, then remove bones and flake the fish.
4. Mix gently and garnish with green onions before serving.

Imo Gohan (Sweet Potato Rice)

Ingredients

- 1 cup short-grain rice
- 1 1/2 cups water
- 1/2 cup Japanese sweet potatoes, diced
- 1/2 tsp salt

Instructions

1. Rinse rice and soak in water for 30 minutes.
2. Add sweet potatoes and salt, then cook as usual.
3. Let sit for 5 minutes before serving.

Matsutake Gohan (Pine Mushroom Rice)

Ingredients

- 1 cup short-grain rice
- 1 1/2 cups dashi broth
- 1/4 cup matsutake mushrooms, sliced
- 1 tbsp soy sauce
- 1 tbsp sake

Instructions

1. Rinse rice and place it in a pot with dashi, soy sauce, and sake.
2. Add matsutake mushrooms and cook as usual.
3. Let sit for 5 minutes before serving.

Hamaguri Gohan (Clam Rice)

Ingredients

- 1 cup short-grain rice
- 1 1/2 cups clam broth (or water)
- 1/2 cup clams, cleaned
- 1 tbsp soy sauce
- 1 tbsp mirin

Instructions

1. Rinse rice and place it in a pot with clam broth, soy sauce, and mirin.
2. Add clams and cook as usual.
3. Let sit for 5 minutes before serving.

Gomoku Gohan (Five-Ingredient Mixed Rice)

Ingredients

- 1 cup short-grain rice
- 1 1/2 cups dashi broth
- 1/4 cup shiitake mushrooms, sliced
- 1/4 cup carrots, julienned
- 1/4 cup bamboo shoots, sliced
- 1/4 cup chicken, diced
- 1 tbsp soy sauce
- 1 tbsp mirin

Instructions

1. Rinse rice and place it in a pot with dashi, soy sauce, and mirin.
2. Add mushrooms, carrots, bamboo shoots, and chicken.
3. Cook as usual and let rest before serving.

Tori Meshi (Chicken Rice)

Ingredients

- 1 cup short-grain rice
- 1 1/2 cups dashi broth
- 1/2 cup chicken, diced
- 1/4 cup shiitake mushrooms, sliced
- 1 tbsp soy sauce
- 1 tbsp mirin

Instructions

1. Rinse rice and place in a pot with dashi, soy sauce, and mirin.
2. Add chicken and mushrooms.
3. Cook as usual and let rest before serving.

Kaki Gohan (Oyster Rice)

Ingredients

- 1 cup short-grain rice
- 1 1/2 cups dashi broth
- 6 fresh oysters, cleaned
- 1 tbsp soy sauce
- 1 tbsp sake
- 1/4 cup green onions, chopped

Instructions

1. Rinse rice and place in a pot with dashi, soy sauce, and sake.
2. Add oysters and cook as usual.
3. Let sit for 5 minutes before serving, then garnish with green onions.

Anago Meshi (Saltwater Eel Rice)

Ingredients

- 1 cup short-grain rice
- 1 1/2 cups dashi broth
- 1 grilled anago (saltwater eel) fillet
- 1 tbsp eel sauce (unagi tare)
- 1/4 cup green onions, chopped

Instructions

1. Rinse rice and place it in a pot with dashi broth.
2. Cook as usual, then top with grilled anago slices.
3. Drizzle with eel sauce and garnish with green onions.

Saba Meshi (Mackerel Rice)

Ingredients

- 1 cup short-grain rice
- 1 1/2 cups dashi broth
- 1 grilled mackerel fillet, flaked
- 1 tbsp soy sauce
- 1 tbsp mirin
- 1/2 tsp grated ginger

Instructions

1. Rinse rice and place in a pot with dashi, soy sauce, and mirin.
2. Cook as usual, then mix in grilled mackerel and ginger.

Shirasu Gohan (Whitebait Rice)

Ingredients

- 1 cup short-grain rice
- 1 1/2 cups water
- 1/2 cup shirasu (boiled whitebait)
- 1 tbsp soy sauce
- 1/4 cup green onions, chopped

Instructions

1. Rinse rice and cook as usual.
2. Serve topped with shirasu and green onions.
3. Drizzle with soy sauce before serving.

Sansai Gohan (Mountain Vegetable Rice)

Ingredients

- 1 cup short-grain rice
- 1 1/2 cups dashi broth
- 1/4 cup shiitake mushrooms, sliced
- 1/4 cup bamboo shoots, sliced
- 1/4 cup fern shoots
- 1 tbsp soy sauce
- 1 tbsp mirin

Instructions

1. Rinse rice and place in a pot with dashi, soy sauce, and mirin.
2. Add mountain vegetables and cook as usual.

Buta Meshi (Pork Rice)

Ingredients

- 1 cup short-grain rice
- 1 1/2 cups dashi broth
- 100g pork belly, sliced
- 1 tbsp soy sauce
- 1 tbsp mirin
- 1/2 tsp grated ginger

Instructions

1. Rinse rice and place in a pot with dashi, soy sauce, and mirin.
2. Add pork belly and cook as usual.
3. Garnish with grated ginger before serving.

Hiyashi Chazuke (Cold Tea Rice)

Ingredients

- 1 bowl cooked rice
- 1/2 cup cold green tea
- 1/4 cup shirasu (whitebait) or grilled salmon flakes
- 1/2 sheet nori, shredded

Instructions

1. Place cooked rice in a bowl.
2. Pour cold green tea over rice.
3. Top with shirasu or salmon and shredded nori.

Yuba Donburi (Tofu Skin Rice Bowl)

Ingredients

- 1 bowl cooked rice
- 1/2 cup yuba (tofu skin), sliced
- 1/2 cup dashi broth
- 1 tbsp soy sauce
- 1 tbsp mirin

Instructions

1. Simmer dashi, soy sauce, and mirin in a pan.
2. Add yuba and heat for 2 minutes.
3. Pour over rice and serve.

Kitsune Donburi (Fried Tofu Rice Bowl)

Ingredients

- 1 bowl cooked rice
- 1/2 cup aburaage (fried tofu), sliced
- 1/2 cup dashi broth
- 1 tbsp soy sauce
- 1 tbsp mirin

Instructions

1. Simmer dashi, soy sauce, and mirin in a pan.
2. Add aburaage and cook for 5 minutes.
3. Serve over rice.

Oyako Donburi (Chicken and Egg Rice Bowl)

Ingredients

- 1/2 cup chicken thigh, sliced
- 1/4 cup onion, sliced
- 1/2 cup dashi broth
- 1 tbsp soy sauce
- 1 tbsp mirin
- 1 egg, beaten
- 1 bowl cooked rice

Instructions

1. Simmer dashi, soy sauce, mirin, and onion in a pan.
2. Add chicken and cook until done.
3. Pour in beaten egg and let it set slightly.
4. Serve over rice.

Tamagotoji Donburi (Scrambled Egg Rice Bowl)

Ingredients

- 2 eggs, beaten
- 1/2 cup dashi broth
- 1 tbsp soy sauce
- 1 tbsp mirin
- 1 bowl cooked rice
- 1/4 cup green onions, chopped

Instructions

1. Heat dashi broth with soy sauce and mirin.
2. Pour in beaten eggs and stir gently until slightly set.
3. Serve over rice and garnish with green onions.

Unadon (Grilled Eel Rice Bowl)

Ingredients

- 1 grilled unagi (freshwater eel) fillet
- 1 bowl cooked rice
- 1 tbsp unagi sauce (unagi tare)
- 1/2 tbsp green onions, chopped

Instructions

1. Slice grilled eel into strips.
2. Serve eel over rice and drizzle with unagi sauce.
3. Garnish with green onions before serving.

Tekka Don (Marinated Tuna Rice Bowl)

Ingredients

- 150g sashimi-grade tuna, sliced
- 1 tbsp soy sauce
- 1/2 tsp mirin
- 1/2 tsp sesame oil
- 1 bowl cooked rice
- 1/2 sheet nori, shredded

Instructions

1. Marinate tuna slices in soy sauce, mirin, and sesame oil for 10 minutes.
2. Serve over rice and garnish with shredded nori.

Niratama Don (Garlic Chive and Egg Rice Bowl)

Ingredients

- 1/2 cup garlic chives, chopped
- 2 eggs, beaten
- 1 tbsp soy sauce
- 1/2 tsp sugar
- 1 bowl cooked rice

Instructions

1. Sauté garlic chives in a pan with soy sauce and sugar.
2. Pour in beaten eggs and cook until set.
3. Serve over rice.

Tororo Gohan (Grated Yam Rice)

Ingredients

- 1/2 cup nagaimo (Japanese yam), grated
- 1 tsp soy sauce
- 1 bowl cooked rice
- 1/2 sheet nori, shredded

Instructions

1. Mix grated yam with soy sauce.
2. Serve over rice and garnish with shredded nori.

Shiso Gohan (Perilla Leaf Rice)

Ingredients

- 1 bowl cooked rice
- 3 shiso leaves, finely chopped
- 1/2 tsp sesame seeds

Instructions

1. Mix shiso leaves and sesame seeds into warm rice.
2. Serve as a side or main dish.

Yaki Onigiri (Grilled Rice Balls)

Ingredients

- 1 cup cooked rice
- 1 tbsp soy sauce
- 1/2 tsp miso paste (optional)

Instructions

1. Shape warm rice into compact balls or patties.
2. Brush lightly with soy sauce or miso paste.
3. Grill until crispy and golden brown.

Ishikari Gohan (Salmon and Miso Rice)

Ingredients

- 1 cup short-grain rice
- 1 1/2 cups dashi broth
- 1 salmon fillet, flaked
- 1 tbsp miso paste
- 1/4 cup green onions, chopped

Instructions

1. Rinse rice and place it in a pot with dashi and miso paste.
2. Add flaked salmon and cook as usual.
3. Garnish with green onions before serving.

Shimeji Gohan (Shimeji Mushroom Rice)

Ingredients

- 1 cup short-grain rice
- 1 1/2 cups dashi broth
- 1/2 cup shimeji mushrooms, trimmed
- 1 tbsp soy sauce
- 1 tbsp mirin

Instructions

1. Rinse rice and place in a pot with dashi, soy sauce, and mirin.
2. Add shimeji mushrooms and cook as usual.

Edamame Gohan (Soybean Rice)

Ingredients

- 1 cup short-grain rice
- 1 1/2 cups water
- 1/2 cup shelled edamame
- 1/2 tsp salt

Instructions

1. Rinse rice and place in a pot with water and salt.
2. Add edamame and cook as usual.

Satsuma Jiru Gohan (Rice with Sweet Potato Soup)

Ingredients

- 1 bowl cooked rice
- 4 cups dashi broth
- 100g pork belly, sliced
- 1/2 cup sweet potatoes, diced
- 1/2 cup miso paste
- 1/4 cup green onions, chopped

Instructions

1. Simmer dashi broth and miso paste.
2. Add pork and sweet potatoes, cooking until tender.
3. Serve alongside a bowl of rice.

Yuba Gohan (Tofu Skin Steamed Rice)

Ingredients

- 1 cup short-grain rice
- 1 1/2 cups dashi broth
- 1/2 cup yuba (tofu skin), torn into strips
- 1 tbsp soy sauce
- 1 tbsp mirin

Instructions

1. Rinse rice and place in a pot with dashi, soy sauce, and mirin.
2. Add yuba and cook as usual.

Katsu Don (Pork Cutlet Rice Bowl)

Ingredients

- 1 pork cutlet (tonkatsu), fried
- 1/2 onion, sliced
- 1/2 cup dashi broth
- 1 tbsp soy sauce
- 1 tbsp mirin
- 1 egg, beaten
- 1 bowl cooked rice

Instructions

1. Simmer dashi, soy sauce, mirin, and onion.
2. Place fried pork cutlet in the pan and pour beaten egg over it.
3. Cook until egg is slightly set, then serve over rice.

Niku Don (Beef Rice Bowl)

Ingredients

- 100g thinly sliced beef
- 1/2 cup dashi broth
- 1 tbsp soy sauce
- 1 tbsp mirin
- 1/4 cup onions, sliced
- 1 bowl cooked rice

Instructions

1. Simmer dashi, soy sauce, mirin, and onions.
2. Add beef and cook until tender.
3. Serve over rice.

Buri Daikon Gohan (Yellowtail and Daikon Rice)

Ingredients

- 1 cup short-grain rice
- 1 1/2 cups dashi broth
- 1/2 cup yellowtail (buri), sliced
- 1/2 cup daikon, sliced
- 1 tbsp soy sauce
- 1 tbsp mirin

Instructions

1. Rinse rice and place in a pot with dashi, soy sauce, and mirin.
2. Add yellowtail and daikon, then cook as usual.

Karasumi Gohan (Salted Mullet Roe Rice)

Ingredients

- 1 bowl cooked rice
- 2 tbsp grated karasumi (salted mullet roe)
- 1/2 sheet nori, shredded

Instructions

1. Serve warm rice in a bowl.
2. Top with grated karasumi and shredded nori.

Satsuma-age Donburi (Fried Fish Cake Rice Bowl)

Ingredients

- 2 pieces satsuma-age (fried fish cake), sliced
- 1/2 cup dashi broth
- 1 tbsp soy sauce
- 1 tbsp mirin
- 1/4 cup onions, sliced
- 1 bowl cooked rice

Instructions

1. Simmer dashi, soy sauce, mirin, and onions.
2. Add sliced satsuma-age and cook for 5 minutes.
3. Serve over rice.

Kibinago Gohan (Silver-Stripe Herring Rice)

Ingredients

- 1 cup short-grain rice
- 1 1/2 cups dashi broth
- 1/2 cup kibinago (silver-stripe herring), cleaned
- 1 tbsp soy sauce
- 1/4 cup green onions, chopped

Instructions

1. Rinse rice and place in a pot with dashi and soy sauce.
2. Add kibinago and cook as usual.
3. Garnish with green onions before serving.

Zuke Don (Marinated Fish Rice Bowl)

Ingredients

- 150g sashimi-grade fish (tuna, salmon, or yellowtail), sliced
- 1 tbsp soy sauce
- 1/2 tsp mirin
- 1/2 tsp sesame oil
- 1 bowl cooked rice
- 1/2 sheet nori, shredded

Instructions

1. Marinate fish in soy sauce, mirin, and sesame oil for 10 minutes.
2. Serve over rice and garnish with shredded nori.

Mentaiko Gohan (Spicy Cod Roe Rice)

Ingredients

- 1 bowl cooked rice
- 1 tbsp mentaiko (spicy cod roe)
- 1/2 sheet nori, shredded

Instructions

1. Serve warm rice in a bowl.
2. Place mentaiko on top and garnish with shredded nori.

Kinoko Meshi (Assorted Mushroom Rice)

Ingredients

- 1 cup short-grain rice
- 1 1/2 cups dashi broth
- 1/2 cup mixed mushrooms (shiitake, enoki, maitake, shimeji), sliced
- 1 tbsp soy sauce
- 1 tbsp mirin

Instructions

1. Rinse rice and place in a pot with dashi, soy sauce, and mirin.
2. Add mushrooms and cook as usual.
3. Let sit for 5 minutes before serving.

Fukagawa Meshi (Clam and Miso Rice)

Ingredients

- 1 cup short-grain rice
- 1 1/2 cups dashi broth
- 1/2 cup clams, cleaned
- 1 tbsp miso paste
- 1 tbsp sake
- 1/4 cup green onions, chopped

Instructions

1. Rinse rice and place in a pot with dashi and sake.
2. Dissolve miso paste in the broth.
3. Add clams and cook as usual.
4. Garnish with green onions before serving.

Saba Misoni Gohan (Miso-Braised Mackerel Rice)

Ingredients

- 1 cup short-grain rice
- 1 1/2 cups dashi broth
- 1 grilled mackerel fillet, flaked
- 1 tbsp miso paste
- 1 tbsp mirin

Instructions

1. Rinse rice and place in a pot with dashi, miso, and mirin.
2. Cook as usual, then mix in flaked mackerel before serving.

Hakata Meshi (Rice with Marinated Raw Fish)

Ingredients

- 1 bowl cooked rice
- 150g sashimi-grade fish (tuna, salmon, yellowtail), sliced
- 1 tbsp soy sauce
- 1/2 tsp mirin
- 1/2 tsp sesame oil
- 1/2 sheet nori, shredded

Instructions

1. Marinate fish slices in soy sauce, mirin, and sesame oil for 10 minutes.
2. Serve over warm rice and garnish with shredded nori.

Gobo Gohan (Burdock Root Rice)

Ingredients

- 1 cup short-grain rice
- 1 1/2 cups dashi broth
- 1/2 cup burdock root (gobo), julienned
- 1 tbsp soy sauce
- 1 tbsp mirin

Instructions

1. Soak burdock root in water for 5 minutes to remove bitterness.
2. Rinse rice and place in a pot with dashi, soy sauce, and mirin.
3. Add burdock root and cook as usual.

Tsukudani Gohan (Rice with Preserved Soy-Simmered Fish)

Ingredients

- 1 bowl cooked rice
- 2 tbsp tsukudani (soy-simmered fish or seaweed)

Instructions

1. Serve warm rice in a bowl.
2. Top with tsukudani and mix before eating.

Shiokara Gohan (Salted Fermented Seafood Rice)

Ingredients

- 1 bowl cooked rice
- 1 tbsp shiokara (fermented squid or seafood)

Instructions

1. Serve warm rice in a bowl.
2. Top with shiokara and mix before eating.

Chahan (Japanese Fried Rice)

Ingredients

- 1 bowl cooked rice (preferably day-old)
- 1 egg, beaten
- 1/4 cup green onions, chopped
- 1/4 cup diced ham or shrimp
- 1 tbsp soy sauce
- 1 tbsp sesame oil

Instructions

1. Heat sesame oil in a pan and scramble the egg.
2. Add green onions and ham, stir-frying for 2 minutes.
3. Add rice and stir well.
4. Drizzle with soy sauce before serving.

Omu Rice (Omelette Rice)

Ingredients

- 1 bowl cooked rice
- 1/4 cup chicken, diced
- 1 tbsp ketchup
- 1 egg, beaten
- 1 tbsp butter

Instructions

1. Sauté chicken in butter, then add rice and ketchup.
2. Cook the beaten egg into an omelet in a separate pan.
3. Place omelet over the rice and serve.

Mochi Gohan (Rice with Sticky Mochi Pieces)

Ingredients

- 1 cup short-grain rice
- 1/2 cup mochi rice (glutinous rice)
- 1 1/2 cups water
- 1/2 cup mochi pieces, diced

Instructions

1. Rinse rice and soak for 30 minutes.
2. Cook rice as usual, adding mochi pieces before steaming.
3. Serve warm.

www.ingramcontent.com/pod-product-compliance
Lightning Source LLC
LaVergne TN
LVHW061953070526
838199LV00060B/4096